The Children of Vaughn

The Story of Professional Baseball in Portland, Oregon (1901-2010)

Round Bend Press Books
Portland, Oregon

Round Bend Press Books
1115 S.W. 11th Ave.
Portland, Oregon

First Edition

Cover photo: Vaughn Street Park

ISBN: 978-0-9850730-7-7

Baseball history—the Portland Beavers—the Pacific Northwest—the Pacific Coast League
Published in the USA

roundbendpressbooks.blogspot.com
roundbendpress@yahoo.com

I see great things in baseball. It's our game - the American game—Walt Whitman

For Dylan Kerr

The Children of Vaughn

The Story of Professional Baseball in Portland, Oregon (1901-2010)

Vaughn Street Park

Forward

This book is partially sourced from a six-part series I wrote for the monthly *Northwest Neighbor* newspaper in 1980. At the time, I delved into the archives of the now defunct *Portland Journal* and *The Oregonian*, reading everything I could find about the early days of baseball in Portland in the microfiche files at Portland's Multnomah County Central Library. The reading repeatedly brought me to the work of legendary Portland sportswriter L.H. Gregory (1885-1975), whose long career included stints at both newspapers and many years as sports editor and columnist at *The Oregonian*. No other writer in Portland had his depth of knowledge, perspective or experience covering baseball in Portland at the time of his death. His reminiscences and game stories provide the bulk of the information in this narrative. The few quotes contained herein, with a couple of exceptions, are gleaned from his articles and are duly noted in the text.

Throughout, readers will discover that I have placed thoughts and possible motives for such thoughts in the minds of several focal characters, as well as in the minds of the fans. I do so unapologetically in the interest of creating something expressly more *historical* than a mere list of events and the common over-reliance on names and dates that is the bane of historicism. Wherever possible, I attempt to fit such material into the context of both the game of baseball and the timeline involved in the story. The level of success I achieved in this endeavor is yours to decide.

For source material beyond 1980, I have also consulted some of my friend Buddy Dooley's scribbling about baseball in Portland, most notably his 2010 essay "Henry Aaron" (from *People, Polemics & Pooh-Pah: Notes from Under the Bar*) regarding David Hersh's purchase of the Beavers. Though no L.H. Gregory, Dooley once had a keen interest in the game. His account of the Hersh years rings true—if somewhat cynical—so I've used him. I've adapted Dooley's facile anecdote about once meeting Aaron from his essay as well.

In addition, I've used online material liberally throughout the text. I can say only that I wish the Internet had been around when I wrote my series long ago. Scholarly historians—and I happen to be a history graduate of Portland State University, so I can verify this—rightfully scorn Wikipedia. The most obvious reason is because the online source is often flawed, or plain wrong. In my research, comparing people and dates attached to my 1980 effort with those I found at Wikipedia and other online sources, there were indeed discrepancies. I have smoothed these over to the best of my ability by assuming that my own original primary-source research trumps the Wiki guys, though I did find instances wherein I was plausibly wrong. I only hope that someone who was around in 1903 doesn't see a mistake I have made and chastise me from the grave.

You as readers are of course free to do that at any time before we all go to baseball heaven.

One final note: The italicized material that I've used to introduce each of the book's chapters is grazed from an article I published in 1979 prior to beginning my original research. I include it here in a hopeful attempt to give the text extra breadth.

Terry Simons
June, 2014
Portland, Oregon

Introduction

Organized amateur baseball arrived in Portland, Oregon in 1866. The first team was spawned from the Front Street offices of the J.W. Cook Company, an awning and tent manufacturer. For the next 17 years, amateur teams in town came and went, along with the businesses that sponsored them.

It is easy to imagine how these early teams might have become magnets for the best players in the community. If you wanted a good, power-hitting first baseman, you'd give him a job in your warehouse and pay him a living wage as he tore up opposing pitchers after work and on weekends. If you needed an accountant in the front office, it might be worth your time to examine both the candidate's math skills and his footwork around second base. As more and more people moved to the growing community, locals might ask where a new arrival was from. The next question could have been, "What position can you play?"

While sponsorship was the key to the success of the best teams in town, not every company was willing or able to take such initiative. The J.W. Cook Company is said to have been highly committed to baseball and its sponsorship role, thus giving the team a competitive advantage and enduring legacy. The company could recruit the best players in town, regardless of where they worked.

That first Portland team called itself the East Portland *Pioneers*, a clever name by any reckoning. By the time of the club's invention Oregon had been a state for all of seven years, and many of the players were exactly what the name claimed. J.W. Cook certainly was, having followed his sons west to help them in business.

The Pioneers' first game of record was against a good team from Oregon City, a horse and buggy ride away. The local papers covered the "match," as it was called among those more accustomed to the old idioms than baseball itself. The match didn't go well, according to one writer who may have not known baseball from cricket. Noting that the J.W. Cook Company got hammered in front of a nice crowd dressed in its Sunday best and furnished picnic-style food by a local restaurateur, he caught the game's idyllic nuances, if not the on-field action. Under clear skies and a warm summer sun, with the ladies dressed in their finest, many fanning themselves under giant elms adjacent to the field, the image conjures up nothing less than a scene worthy of Norman Rockwell—a painting of a town falling in love with Whitman's *American game.*

Interest in baseball grew quickly in Portland and nearby communities. In February 1868, the East Portland Pioneers led the effort to create an association of amateur clubs for "gentlemen." The rules prohibited the use of professional players and, likely, foul language. The Pioneers were joined in the association by two other Portland baseball clubs—the *Monograms* and the *Highlanders*—the Clackamas/Oregon City club, and a club based across the Columbia River from Portland in Vancouver—the *Occidentals*. Others joined over the years as the association expanded into Idaho.

It was only a matter of time before someone would make a move to capitalize on the game, as had happened on the East Coast and in the Midwest.

Beginnings (1883-1900)

Easter Sunday, 1979. The day is overcast, dark, threatening. Down on the Tartan Turf stadium floor a KXL van moves slowly onto the field. We are between games of a baseball doubleheader at Civic Stadium. The resurrected Portland Beavers have just beaten the Spokane Indians 4-0 in the first game, their fourth straight win. They are undefeated. The season is young.

The year was 1883 and Portland was growing increasingly ripe for a professional team. Joe Buchtel, who had managed the Pioneers for years, decided to create another Portland-based team and began to explore the possibility of using full-time and semi-professional players. A talented player/manager whose working life included turns as a fireman and railroad man, Buchtel wanted to stay close to the game after his playing days ended.

He called his new team the *Willamettes*, after the river that runs through the heart of the fertile Willamette Valley and downtown Portland. By 1890 he'd changed the team's name to the *Webfeet*, a nod to Oregon's long rainy season and waterfowl population, and helped initiate the first semi-professional league in the Pacific Northwest. For the next three years the tiny Pacific

14

Northwest League struggled to maintain its equilibrium in a highly volatile economy. The league also featured teams in Spokane, Seattle and Tacoma, playing a full and rigorous schedule, even venturing as far south as Sacramento, San Francisco and San Jose for interleague games with members of the longer-established and only slightly healthier California League.

At the height of what is known as the *Panic of 1893*, the league collapsed at mid-season.

Portland won the Pacific Northwest League's inaugural championship series, but its initial success wasn't enough to sustain ticket sales in Portland. The Webfeet and the other clubs called it a day in light of the miserable economy.

A brief reprisal took hold three years later, in 1896. The comeback also failed and the league folded once more. Portland's record before the collapse was 19-9, a dismally short season by any standard.

As much as people in the region loved baseball, most of them, potential owners and fans alike, simply couldn't afford the game. In Portland's case, the club also lacked the sort of facilities that draw fans and enhance the experience of watching baseball.

But Portland's time would come, and it happened as the nineteenth century ended. The 110-year history of fully self-sufficient professional baseball in Portland Oregon was about to begin in earnest.

Comeback (1900-1903)

Portland's pitchers have thrown extremely well. An uprising in the 5th inning was put down when a pair of hard liners were squeezed by Beaver infielders. The five-hundred fans love the action!

William H. Lucas was a Montana baseball man, the president of the Montana State League. In 1900, he saw the Pacific Northwest as fertile ground and dreamed of expanding the professional game to the seemingly cursed region. Hungry for bigger success beyond Montana, he organized a meeting of well-heeled businessmen from the area to explore the potential of once more reviving the professional circuit in the Pacific Northwest.

Three successful Portlanders agreed the timing was correct and quickly jumped aboard, along with interested friends in Seattle and Tacoma. The Portland principals were Max Fleischer, C.A. Whitmore and Frank Devers, and the Pacific Northwest League was reborn, this time as a fully-autonomous professional circuit. There soon followed the construction of a new ball park, a gem named Vaughn Street Park. It was built at the edge of Portland's burgeoning Northwest Industrial

Area and immediately became an attractive destination for the city's baseball lovers. Accessible by trolley from all over the city, the park made Portlanders proud. It also attracted the gazes of some of region's best players and biggest financiers.

With the creation of Vaughn Street Park, which many believed to be one of the best stadiums on the West Coast, Portland began to stick out. A kid from Kansas who had played a couple of years of semi-professional ball in his home state caught the eye of Lucas and his partners. The kid's name was Joe Tinker, a smooth-fielding infielder and polished hitter with a bright future. Lucas called his team the *Webfoots* and signed Tinker to play third base in the shiny new park. A bold stroke, it piqued the interest of Portland's fans and others nationally. (Tinker hit .290 for the Webfoots in 1901. The next year he would join the Chicago Cubs and eventually, along with Johnny Evers and Frank Chance, lead the Cubbies to their first and last dynasty.)

As Tinker was making a name for himself in the upstart west, baseball's businessmen nationally were plotting the game's future by creating a comprehensive new association that would consolidate the game's pecking order. It was the beginning of the permutations that would eventually create the structure of the game as it exists today—an official system of major and minor leagues. East of the Mississippi, baseball's power dynamics represented a long-established though chaotic order. As people and the game spread westward, new territories and opportunities sprang up. Baseball had entered a new marketing phase, evolving from steady improvements in transportation, new and improved facilities, and expanding population centers. The Vaughn Street jewel became emblematic. The stadium brought interest, a nice capacity, a lush field, and a future for baseball in Portland.

The *National Association of Professional Baseball Leagues* arose in 1901, displacing the *National Association of Base Ball Players*, founded in 1871, as the predominate organization in the game. It also signaled the beginning of the end of player-centric control of baseball's finances.

The *NAPBL* quickly formalized the game's growth boundaries by creating a classification system that altered the way players were scouted, signed and developed. This was resultant of an ongoing power struggle at baseball's highest levels in the populace east. The teams that would eventually comprise the National and American Leagues were battling each other for control of the game's resources. The feuds had hurt upstart leagues, which were powerless against the wealthier clubs whenever the big fish decided to raid a lesser league for both players and territorial control. The new system gave minor-league baseball a much-needed structure and legal method of fighting baseball's monopolistic interests. It helped establish both a judicial means and a compensatory method that aided the increasingly popular baseball business by clarifying contractual obligations and territorial rights.

In Portland young Joe Tinker, a much-coveted player, found a secure home and a rock-solid contract wherein all the interests involved were forced to deal with a new paradigm. It assured that Tinker couldn't merely walk away when the Chicago Cubs called. If the Cubs wanted him, they'd have to buy his contract. (This dynamic would change again with the influx of "free-agency" years later, which further altered baseball's contractual system and strengthened the hands of the game's best players.)

When the dust settled and *NAPBL's* ideas were enacted, Portland's Webfoots and the revived Pacific Northwest League became a Class-B organization.

The business of baseball was definitely "on," and for the next 110 years Portland would play a significant role in the game's growth, while never achieving the perennial dream of joining the modern major leagues.

Introducing the Pacific Coast League

Five-hundred fans? You're kidding me. Has the threat of rain and a televised Blazer basketball game kept the crowd away in droves? Or does this town just not care about baseball anymore?

Heretofore, baseball's power structure had been centered in the large population communities of the East and upper Midwest, with players being the dominant structural force. The West had its centers of interest as well, mainly in the San Francisco and Los Angeles regions. The California League in its original manifestation, like the fledgling Pacific Northwest League, constantly battled the economy of baseball, but those centers of interest were growing up quickly. Hope lay in the future and a yet newer business model.

William Lucas sought to reorganize and expand the Pacific Northwest League. The Montanan had a particular fondness for two of the franchises in his old Montana League. Butte and Helena were good baseball towns, known commodities, so he brought them into the revived league and its Portland-based sphere of influence. As 1901 wound down, he sought even greater territorial expansion and began negotiations with the owners of several California teams in an effort to absorb the larger markets in the southland.

A great deal of genuflection and bargaining took shape as the Pacific Northwest League run by Lucas engaged in talks with competition in California during the winter of 1901-02. With the month of March upon them and the expected beginning of a new season rapidly approaching, the California and Pacific Northwest Leagues were in disarray as various interests jockeyed for position. Even as Lucas plotted to bring one or more of the California teams into his league, owners there were engaged in a similar plot to absorb Lucas' territory into their own orbit. The Californians coveted Seattle and Portland, but were less enthralled with the Montana connections. The reason was fairly obvious, even as the stubborn Lucas made a last-ditch effort to keep Butte and Helena in play. Though both great baseball towns, neither was monetarily enticing from the standpoint of potential ticket sales and travel logistics. The California owners, accustomed to bigger ball parks and the closer proximity of the league's teams, held the stronger hand. Their business model reflected the lessons absorbed by watching the eastern teams, which had grown up fast and now dominated the game.   Travel to Montana's hinterlands coupled with the smallish and inadequate facilities there simply wouldn't work economically.

The 1902 season played out without expansion or realignment as the owners in California and Lucas stood pat. Without Joe Tinker, who had moved on to the Cubs, Portland finished fourth in the Pacific Northwest League's second season.

When that winter's round of baseball talks commenced in December 1902, the owner of the San Francisco Seals, Henry Harris, finally got through to Lucas. A new league as Harris envisioned it would rival anything on the other coast if handled properly. That meant that Portland and Seattle, furnished with high-capacity ball parks, could and should be part of a new baseball dynamic, an entity called the Pacific Coast League that would begin play in 1903. Its initial membership would include four California teams— Harris' San Francisco Seals, the Oakland Oaks, the Los Angeles Angels and Sacramento Senators. Portland and Seattle would make six.

Comprised of cities large enough to support the new league and a better caliber of ball player, the PCL might become a major league in-waiting. The prospective teams were fixed up with the proper stadiums, travel infrastructure, and hotel accommodations suitable for long days and nights on the road.

What more could you ask for?

Struggling Years (1903-1905)

The KXL van moves hauntingly to mid-field. In its coffin-dark interior are eggs. Plastic eggs. Plastic, multi-colored Easter eggs filled with embryonic gift certificates that will metamorphose into colored televisions and digital clocks at mid-week.

The first owners of the PCL (designated a Class-A league by the *NAPBL*) Portland *Browns* were brothers Fred and Ben Ely. They purchased the Webfoots from the recalcitrant William Lucas and immediately changed the team's name in their first act of annoying local fans.

William Frederick "Bones" Ely was a former major-league shortstop nearing the end of a long and accomplished career that included a couple of seasons playing for the St. Louis Browns, which must have given him an idea of what to call his new team. He'd finished his major-league career for the Washington Senators in 1902 at age 40.

Bones Ely held down shortstop and managerial duties in 1903 as his brother Ben worked the front office. Neither seemed to have much acumen for the business side of the game, and clearly an over-the-hill shortstop wasn't likely to excite, so ticket sales at Vaughn Street lagged after opening day. It's common knowledge that winners put fannies in the seats, and the 1903 Browns were pretty bad by all accounts, finishing fifth in the inaugural PCL season. They started poorly and struggled throughout the 200-game season. (If you think today's baseball season is too long like this author does, imagine baseball in its formative years, when 200-game seasons were not uncommon in the era of rail travel and less-than-luxuriant hotel accommodations.)

The Ely brothers lost their shirts along with most of their games in 1903. Meanwhile, another former major-league player from the East Coast saw an opportunity in Portland. His uncle was a Vancouver, WA superior court judge named William McCredie, and the player's name was Walter McCredie.

Judge McCredie had been keeping close watch on what was transpiring across the Columbia in Portland, where he saw that the Elys were in obvious trouble. His first observation was that Bones Ely wasn't a very good manager. His second observation was that brother Ben was lost at sea when it came to promoting the game and finding the right players for the team. It would only be a matter of time, Judge McCredie told his nephew, before the Elys would have to sell.

The brothers hung on for another year, however, as Bones Ely turned the team over to another manager, hiring Dave "Dug" Dugdale away from the PCL's Seattle franchise. Portland's fans liked the popular Dugdale at first because he vowed to create a more youthful team, cutting loose many of the worn out veterans who made up the 1903 roster. Dug was true to his word, bringing in a handful of new young players, but fans soon realized the team hadn't really improved because some of the new players were not really ready for the PCL's level of play. They were certainly game and projected well for the future, and they could run circles around the old guys, but they were green and couldn't hit. The youngsters started slow and ended worse—as in the league's cellar. Weeks before the 1904 campaign ended, Dugdale resigned and moved back to Seattle.

Vaughn Street was empty of all but the diehards, and the Ely brothers were ready to sell.

The McCredies (1905-1921)

Young baseball promoter David Hersh is walking two steps to the van's rear, smoking a thick cigar. The cigar has to be big to fit the kid's image and fulfill his dreams, his vision of fielding a MBL team in Portland by 1982. David Hersh is having fun, just like the hundred or more kids who have streamed down to the field to hunt Easter eggs. He's just 23 years old, the youngest baseball team owner in the land. The cigar has to be big, you see?

Before baseball's modern era and the solidification of the two major leagues—the National and American—it was not uncommon at all for former players to seek out and find baseball ownership opportunities as their playing careers waned. Whereas today's retirees turn to the stock market and other investments, and often times coaching, as well as radio and television jobs—if they have to work at all—the old timers bought clubs as a way to stay in the game. Today's big-league owners come from the billionaires' class, and while top ex-players might end up in management, public relations and team development, few opportunities for ownership at the highest level arise for washed up superstars. Baseball became dynastic once it became super lucrative. Owners tend to stick around and pass the baby off to heirs, or sell to other billionaires in low-risk, big-profit style.

Bones Ely was a .258 lifetime hitter, likely at the top-end of the wage scale as a player over a long career, but his pockets were obviously not deep. After two losing seasons he and his brother were forced out to find new jobs. The soon-to-be new owners, William and Walter McCredie, likely had deeper pockets, and it is an undisputed fact that they were better baseball men. Walter played in the outfield for Dug Dugdale during the 1904 PCL season after a stint with the Brooklyn *Superbas* in 1903. With his uncle watching him play and whispering in his ear, they hatched a plan and made an offer to the Elys that William McCredie would later describe as "peanuts."

When the 1905 season rolled around, Walter McCredie was the 29 year-old player/manager of the Portland club.

The new owners' success didn't happen overnight, but in baseball terms the team turned things around fairly quickly. The youth movement that Bones and Ben Ely and David Dugdale initiated the previous season was the right move; they simply gambled on the wrong players, a number of whom Judge McCredie counted as overpaid problem children. The McCredies didn't have the time to rearrange the roster before their inaugural season was underway. The usual fall to the cellar awaited them.

The McCredies also had changed the name of the team to the Giants, even though there were already three well-known teams in the country with that team name.

While Portland's first three seasons in the PCL hadn't been great successes, the community had its favorites among the players, enough so that over the winter, prior to 1906, the diehards began to protest when the McCredies started making changes.

First, as a method of appeasing the home town crowd, the second-year owners held a naming contest for the team. That would work in their favor. If the franchise was going to re-invent itself, it should lose the Giants handle Judge McCredie figured after hearing fans' complaints about the name. The fans' involvement in a newspaper vote would be good public relations as well. The naming suggestions came in and the fans voted for the *Beavers.*

As nice as the renaming gambit was for the organization, 1906 soon brought some ill-will in the McCredies' direction, however. Before the season started, they began to slash the salaries of some of their more unproductive players, even the very popular ones. The top salary in the PCL at the time, mandated by the league, was $2,700 on a six-month contract. Several Giants were making that figure, and the McCredies had evidence they were overpaid. They hadn't earned the money in 1905 because they hadn't won anything, the McCredies reasoned. Judge McCredie asked several "stars" to play for half their previous year's salaries, which naturally created some clubhouse tension that inconveniently spilled into the community and the local papers. The *Oregon Journal* editorialized on 18 March, 1906: "The cutting of players' salaries is false economy."

Referring to the three-tiered pay structure of the time, the non-bylined editorial said:

> "The only ones who appear to be in Class A from the standpoint of salary are President McCredie, Manager McCredie, Secretary Shepard, and Groundskeeper, Higgins. It is interesting to note that nearly $8,000 of the money made during the coming season will be paid to management, aside from profits that may be made."

The McCredies ignored the criticism. Two of the team's biggest stars, Jud Smith and Bill Flood, refused to play for them, essentially walking out on their contracts. According to their critics, the new owners had ruined baseball in Portland in just their second year at the helm. Critics from Front Street to the West Hills believed it to be true.

Judge McCredie was a good businessman. He knew what he was doing, especially with young Walter at his side. They used spring training in Stockton, CA to build a new club fashioned more on effort than egoism, and the onus fell on Walter to select the players to bring home to Portland and a new season. Judge McCredie also emphasized good character in a game that had a lot of the bad variety.

Little hope was given among the writers covering the team in Stockton that the Beavers would rise above the fourth-place finish of 1905. Heavens, the team's best two players had just walked out the door, hadn't they?

Oregon Journal sportswriter L.H. Gregory, beginning his long career in Portland, reported a lack of depth on the mound, weak hitters and questionable speed. In what may have been a mocking tone, he wrote, "All the Giants have made a big hit with the Stockton public.

They are a fine, sober and gentlemanly lot and nothing but words of praise are heard for the boys on all sides."

One presumes the old Browns of past seasons may not have been the most sober and gentlemanly figures in Portland, and that the writer's words were meant as much as a poke at the McCredies as team news for the reading public. Was Judge McCredie a moralist himself, intent on creating a roster in his own image? One would think so, given his title and bearing. And wouldn't that have rubbed off on the younger McCredie? It likely had.

Gregory continued with this fine subtlety: "Some of the boys have made great hits with the ladies, and when the Webfoots pull their stakes they will leave many saddened hearts behind."

Beyond laconically referring to the team's old nickname, the writer appeared to be continuing his sarcastic streak. This group of players might not be any good, but gosh they were sure nice guys. Perhaps that is all the McCredies were really interested in?

And then there was this cynical portrait of the team's general demeanor:

> "Several of the players pass much of their
> spare time down at the skating rinks.

There is hardly a night that you can't find shortstop Sweeney at the Pavilion rink. The roller skating has caught Stockton by storm and the players have caught the fever good and plenty."

Portland baseball had turned very wholesome indeed under the McCredies' guidance. The writer went on to pick the San Francisco Seals to win the fourth PCL championship.

As it turned out Walter McCredie, like his uncle, knew what he was doing. He also had an eye for real talent. The team split the opening eight-game series in Fresno, an expansion PCL team. The highlight had been an opening-game two-hitter by one of the team's young nobodies.

From Fresno the team moved to Oakland, where after the opening game of the series with the Oaks they were in bed—or should have been if they wanted to play for the McCredies—at 5:12 a.m. on April 18, 1906.

The great *San Francisco Earthquake*, aside from creating devastation all around the San Francisco Bay Area, immediately threw the Pacific Coast League into economic peril. San Francisco and Oakland were among the largest markets in the league. The PCL's revenue-sharing scheme suddenly collapsed like buildings in both cities, though the damage in Oakland would soon be determined to be minimal. Thanks to its uncrowded design and first-rate fire department and community activism, the many fires in the city were quickly quashed.

Closely-built and densely crowded San Francisco was another story. Much of the city burned to the ground. Within hours after the quake, Oakland was graciously taking in the many survivors and homeless from across the bay.

The league's San Francisco dates and some of Oakland's early on after the quake had to be abandoned, of course, creating a league-wide dilemma. The Seals, a very popular club, were the kingpins of the PCL. The new league was after all Seals' owner Henry Harris' idea to begin with. The revenue scheme which he had wisely negotiated to bring top-flight baseball to the West Coast's biggest cities had made it all possible. The Seals were a perennial power. They drew the largest crowds day in and day out.

Where would the lost revenue for those games come from? A quick survey of the owners saw a panicky split down the middle, with several clubs threatening to save the season by reorganizing and joining other leagues ASAP. While the dismemberment of the Class-B California and Northwest Leagues and creation of the PCL had stripped the west's minor leagues of their numbers, they were still trying to do business and were scheduled to start their seasons in the near future. Was there time enough for PCL teams to jump aboard the lesser leagues and save the season?

There were arguments pro and con whether or not to take such a route. On the positive side, a new and sudden realignment might very well save the season, even if it meant dropping a level or two in terms of competition. While Class-B ticket sales wouldn't be overwhelming because of the smaller parks in some of the league's communities, the interest of the fans could be held, and something more monetarily substantial than nothing would theoretically trickle in. Perhaps it was time to rebuild, heal and look to the future rather than the present? The negative side of the equation told another story. Several of the Class-B teams were new enterprises that arose out of the dismantling of the California and Northwest Leagues by the PCL, so there was already a glut in some markets that could ill-afford

37

one. Portland was such a case. A Class-B team built from scratch had popped up in the city soon after the Browns joined the PCL. In fact, that team shared Vaughn Street Park with the PCL club, playing its home games when the big club was on the road. A similar dynamic was playing out in other cities along the coast, most notably in Los Angeles where numerous lower-classified teams fought it out for customers.

Judge McCredie was adamantly opposed to dropping down to force a direct competition with the city's new Class-B team, which was in fact a team—the Portland *Pippins*—that he'd helped form as a quasi-farm team for his Beavers. Portland just wasn't big enough for two teams to co-exist by playing a similar schedule against teams from the old, reworked territory—now called the Pacific National League.

Portland needed Los Angeles. It needed Oakland and San Francisco and Seattle. It needed Fresno, the new PCL expansion franchise. Those teams drew fans to Vaughn Street because all of them featured a better brand of baseball. The fans wanted the big names and big teams to roll into town. For the McCredies, nothing else would do. They weren't in the business to piddle around in Portland. The McCredies wanted nothing whatsoever to do with Butte and Helena, no matter what the consequences. The majority of PCL owners and fans agreed.

When Judge McCredie prevailed in the PCL talks about the future, he finally earned the trust of Portlanders. Under his leadership, the league created an altered fiscal structure that bought the clubs time, and the Seals determined to play their home games in Oakland. The owners' first realization was that none of them would make the kind of money they were counting on at the season's start. Yes, some of them would have a harder time paying the bills than others, but deferred payments, loans, salary cuts and mutual support could enhance their plans for the near future. In essence, the shared revenue would necessarily take a dive with the league's most lucrative team sidelined, but too much was at stake—including the future viability of the league—to abandon ship so early in the game. Now was a time for sharing and planning, not cutthroat business. Sacrifice was in order.

The Pacific Coast League clung to life.

Turning it Around

Easter Sunday. No rain. Yet. We need a dome in Portland. The 1982 Beavers will need a dome to bring Major League Baseball to the city. Last year, when Leo Ornest owned the Beavers, rainouts contributed to the team's demise. In a comic book ending to a wet season, PCL officials cancelled the playoffs in September, negating whatever tenuous meaning there was to the season to begin with.

Portlanders forgave the McCredies their past sins and accepted them as the saviors of the PCL, and thus the high level of baseball they'd come to expect in their town. As the 1906 club played on that summer it surprisingly started winning a lot of games, which further bolstered the McCredies' reputations. The young, heretofore unknown players were better than imagined, and people finally understood that Walter McCredie could indeed find and groom talent.

L.H. Gregory wrote in 1944, ten years after Walter McCredie's death at 59:

> "He stood six-two, weighed a slim 180, and carried himself as erect as a forest fir. He had fine broad shoulders and a deep chest. But the unforgettable thing was his face. It was broad and ruddy, with high

wide forehead, a well-formed but hawklike Roman nose, and a stern and commanding chin. In repose, his features were grim and unyielding, somehow remindful to our imaginative, youthful admiration of those austere 'Roundheads' of Oliver Cromwell, but it could, and often did, light up with an engaging smile. On the field he was stern, merciless and so high-strung that he champed like a nervous horse. He played right field in those days, and there are still old-timers who can tell you about the path he wore out there as he stalked back and forth, never still. At bat in a 'clutch' situation he was positively deadly. How he could hit! He was so determined to win that nothing stopped him. He would have badgered the devil to win a ball game."

Walter McCredie was, as Gregory went on to describe him, a disciplinarian and a teacher who took the game very seriously—a consummate professional. He was a rollercoaster of emotion on the field and in the clubhouse. He was the kind of manager who could insult and maim with his criticism when one of his young, developing players erred in the field. But he could also take the same kid out to dinner that night and coolly discuss why he'd been angered and why the kid must play better—how the kid *could* play better.

He was what is commonly referred to as a "player's manager," which is another way of saying a patient teacher who never quit on his pupils.

"He maintained the gift of the funny ending," wrote Gregory.

The Beavers won the 1906 PCL pennant, finishing 115-60. The winning percentage (.657) stood for 28 years as a league record, until the Los Angeles Angels broke it in 1934. The winning total might have been even higher, but the McCredies sold the contracts of catcher Larry McLean and their winningest pitcher, Bill "Vinegar" Essick, to the Cincinnati Reds late in the season, when the championship was already assured.

As great a year as 1906 was, because the club stormed from nowhere to win the PCL, the McCredies' peak years were still ahead. In total, their reign would last 17 seasons. They would win pennants four more times, in 1910 and 1911, and in 1913 and 1914.

The baseball business in Portland was, finally, very good.

In 1917, upon the United States' entry into World War I, play in the PCL was suspended due to travel restrictions imposed by the federal government. The

McCredies kept the franchise operative by dropping down to the Class-B Pacific Coast International League.

In other words, it took a war for the McCredies to finally consign their team to an inferior league.

By the end of the era, according to Gregory, Walter McCredie had mellowed. His playing days were long over and he never really liked managing from the bench. Walter and Judge McCredie were evidently both displeased with the changes surrounding the game by 1921. It was time to sell the franchise.

Walter McCredie took a job with Seattle, and later became a roving scout with the Detroit Tigers.

He reappeared in Portland in 1934 to manage a final season, this time for his old friend Tom Turner's Beavers. At the time, McCredie was sick and aware that death loomed.

He died midway through the season on the eve of a commemorative day in his honor at Vaughn Street Park. It was a sad ending to a special and historical career in professional baseball, as well as the end of the most spectacular era in Portland's baseball history.

The Warring Years (1921-1924)

David Hersh has talked from the start of staying for the long haul in Portland—unlike Leo Ornest, who took the Beavers to Spokane after last season. Picked up and left town, probably because he figured the business climate is better there, along with the weather.

Portland had won five pennants in nine years. It had arrived as a baseball town.

But as quickly as fame and fortune came it was swept away. Spiraling downward, the Beavers managed to finish no higher than fourth in the seven ensuing seasons after the McCredies' final, 1914 championship. In their final two seasons, 1920 and 1921, they finished dead last.

Along came a young woolen-goods broker named William Klepper. A dedicated member of the Elks and a recognized dandy, he'd put together an organization comprised of other influential Elks in Seattle during the early years of the PCL, bringing the franchise back from near-insolvency. He had been the Seattle club's president. Now it was his turn to become a majority owner of a PCL club. The McCredies sold the Beavers to

Klepper and a group of Portland Elks for $150,000. The controlling shares went to Klepper himself.

Klepper made an immediate blunder that would, in three short years, cause him to leave baseball for a time. An aggressive businessman, he would knowingly break a few of the gentlemanly rules of organized baseball as he set about revitalizing the Portland situation. In Seattle, under Klepper's watch, there was a field manager named Bill "Duke" Kenworthy who was highly coveted around the PCL and beyond—a proven winner. Klepper thought Kenworthy the best man available to replace Walter McCredie as manager in Portland. The only problem was Kenworthy wasn't really available. He was under contract as a player/manager with Seattle in a deal Klepper himself had initiated prior to buying the Beavers.

No problem, the new owner reasoned, because he had a plan. To free Kenworthy of his Seattle contract Klepper, who still worked for Seattle for a short time after purchasing the Portland club, first gave the manager his unconditional release—that is, he fired him. Then Klepper resigned his position in the Seattle organization. Assuming he and Kenworthy were both free to carry on with the development of the new Portland team, Klepper gave his favorite manager a new contract—this one with the Beavers. In addition, Kenworthy was awarded shares of Portland's stock.

Watching these developments, after having them called to his attention by Seattle's angry management, was the first commissioner of baseball, whom the owners of the teams in the National and American Leagues had hired to help clean up their game. The famous 1919 "Black Sox" gambling scandal surrounding "Shoeless" Joe Jackson and the Chicago White Sox, as well as other less-famous instances of malfeasance, had given baseball a black eye nationwide. (Recall the McCredies' disillusionment with the game at the time of their sale of the Beavers.)

Delivered unto the baseball establishment by the establishment itself, Judge Kenesaw Mountain Landis was supposedly the new face of honesty in the game. Appointed by President Theodore Roosevelt to the federal judiciary in Ohio in 1905, he had made any number of important decisions in the past, including overseeing the anti-trust trials that broke up John D. Rockefeller's Standard Oil Company in 1906. Ironically Landis, who had been a corporate attorney prior to joining the bench, was thought to have been a friend of big business. Sometimes he was.

He would become a great friend of the big-boy baseball business no doubt, but Rockefeller and others found out something about Landis eventually. He had a stubborn streak if something disturbed him. Judge Landis came down hard on corporate greed, draft dodgers, antiwar protesters and black people, in no particular order.

Landis would serve as baseball commissioner from his appointment in 1920 to his death in 1944. He is generally credited with blocking early efforts to integrate baseball. In that regard, he fit nicely into the American scene BJR (Before Jackie Robinson) as he frequently noted that the "Negro" was doing fine without the mingling of the races in Major League Baseball.

Unlike Branch Rickey, he cared naught that Negro leagues held many very good players that might help a team in the National or American League to a pennant. For their part, neither did many of the big-league owners, for some unfathomable reason.

Judge Landis was, everybody noted, a "character."

Baseball was filled with characters at the time, most of them as racist as Landis.

Judge Landis also had power, though in the early stages of baseball's biggest growth years—the Ruth, Gehrig and DiMaggio eras—and throughout Landis' tenure, it wasn't always clear how much. Even as he claimed empire and feuded with Babe Ruth, seeking to put the kibosh on Ruth's off-season barnstorming tours.

Baseball had hired Landis for another important reason: he viewed labor relations on the corporate side, having often argued that baseball players were not laborers and thus unprotected by any pro-labor rulings then working their way through U.S. courts.

When the Seattle and Portland feud came to his attention, the role of the baseball commissioner was yet to be fully and legally determined, though Landis quickly demanded control. The Klepper/Kenworthy affair helped clarify issues by placing PCL and Minor League Baseball in direct confrontation with Major League Baseball, and subsequently into the courts.

Before Klepper's first Portland team played a game, the waters became deep and murky with legal threats and counter threats. Two weeks into the 1922 season

Landis ruled Kenworthy unworthy and pulled him out of his Portland uniform. The manager/part owner was forced to the sidelines, where he watched Portland's opening day with a mob of 20,000, the largest crowd to ever watch a game in Vaughn Street Park. (The McCredies had, in the middle of their glory years, added 12,000 new seats to the stadium, making Vaughn one of the largest ball parks in the league.)

As for Klepper, Landis warned that something would also have to be done to punish him for raiding the Seattle club. That decision came down at baseball's winter meetings in 1922, when Landis barred Klepper from baseball.

The decision would take time to play out in the courts, of course, because Klepper filed a lawsuit. In the meantime, he went about his business.

Survival

Today's baseball fans aren't interested in mediocrity. People come to the park to watch their team win. They demand excellence and are not interested in losing or losers. Americans know baseball. If your team loses its locals the gig is up. Time to go.

What had happened was that the first baseball commissioner had clipped the wings of minor-league authority. Remember the *National Association of Professional Baseball Leagues* formed in 1901, an organization created expressly to confront the power of the big boys while protecting the rights of poorer minor-league organizations? Where did its influence and interests now fit in given the decisions of Landis? The *NAPBL* in fact sanctioned the hire of Landis. In subsequent years it wasn't always clear if that had been the right thing to do, considering the commissioner's dominating power over not just the major leagues, but all of baseball. Given the new leader's role, was he really any less corrupt than "Shoeless Joe" Jackson? Those were good, solid American business questions. What could Klepper do, given his investment, but slog on?

Despite the troubles he'd brought upon himself in mishandling the Kenworthy hiring, Klepper proved to be an adept baseball man in one fashion—he knew how to make money. No sooner had he forked over the $150,000 for the Beavers than he began to wheel and deal, selling young and talented players on the open market. Though some of these players had been unproductive during the McCredies' decline, a few of baseball's overlords knew and believed in the players. Baseball is a gamble on arms and potential in general— *win some lose some* is a maxim. A player can be a rising star one minute and a dog the next. Conversely, dogs sometimes turn into proficient contributors, if seldom stars. That's baseball.

Klepper sold a pair of underperforming and losing pitchers—Oregon-bred phenom Herman Pillette, who had pitched one game for the Cincinnati Reds as a 17 year-old in 1917, and Portland native Sylvester Johnson—to the Detroit Tigers for $40,000 cash and seven players. The deal shocked the baseball world until Pillette came through in 1923, winning 19 games for the Tigers. Unfortunately, that was his high-water mark, and by 1928 he was out of baseball. "Syl" Johnson would enjoy a journeyman's career with the Tigers, St.

Louis and Cincinnati, where he pitched his final game in 1940 at age 39.

Klepper wheeled again. From Seattle he low-balled a deal for local left-handed pitcher George "Rube" Walberg, used him during the 1922 season, and then sold his contract to the New York Giants and John J. McGraw for $75,000. As it turned out, McGraw would change his mind about Walberg after a few outings and returned him to Portland. McGraw agreed to forfeit his $20,000 down payment on the pitcher to get out of the deal.

Next, Klepper offered Walberg to Philadelphia's Connie Mack, who got the lefty for a more palatable $10,000. Walberg worked out well for Mack, garnering an average of 16 wins a season for the Athletics from 1926 to 1932. He also earned the ignominy of being Babe Ruth's whipping post, allowing a record 17 home runs to the Babe lifetime. Walberg pitched in five World Series over his 10-year career in Philly, going 1-1.

As he was shaping the deal with Mack, Klepper returned third baseman Sammy Hale to Detroit. He was one of the seven throw-in players Klepper had received in the Pillette/Johnson deal. The Tigers sent Hale off to

Mack's Athletics soon thereafter—likely recouping the $40,000 they'd given Klepper for him.

Sammy Hale was a very good player, a lifetime .302 hitter, and Klepper wasn't making many friends among Portland's fans or other PCL owners by running the Beavers in his aggressive manner. He was, many thought, diluting the product on the West Coast.

Baseball had become the *art of the deal* way before Donald Trump used the title, and as much as the PCL complained the truth was Klepper was simply beating the other owners at their game.

If you have the idea the new Portland owner was in the game for the money, you are correct. Other deals brought in significant cash totals, enough that Klepper quickly recouped his original investment in the club.

Baseball players were meat, commodities, it was clear. Klepper felt that way, but so did Landis. It would take many years before free agency and contract law sorted out baseball's labor rules and turned the game into what it is today—a unionized league.

The three years of Klepper's reign were tempestuous. No sooner had Kenworthy been given the boot by

Landis than Klepper's second choice to manage the Beavers was also axed by the commissioner.

Albert Wentworth Demaree was a solid journeyman pitcher who played from 1912-1919 for the New York Giants, Philadelphia Athletics, Chicago Cubs and Boston Braves before hanging them up at age 35. He finished his career at 80-72 with a 2.77 ERA.

Klepper thought Demaree was his man of the future. Landis disagreed. To this day it is uncertain why, though one theory has it that Landis was simply being vindictive because Klepper was suing him.

Writer Robert C. Cottrell dug up this Landis quote for his 2002 book, *Blackball, the Black Sox, and the Babe*:

> "Now that I am in baseball, just watch the game I play. If I catch any crook in baseball, the rest of his life is going to be a pretty hot one. I'll go to any means and to anything possible to see that he gets a real penalty for his offense."

The *Eight Men Out* in the "Black Sox" scandal discovered Landis wasn't kidding. Their lifetime bans held throughout their remaining days. Many others felt Landis' wrath as well, just as Klepper felt it during his first season in Portland.

In all, Klepper employed five managers in the three seasons he owned the Beavers. The first two were the only ones fired by Landis, but both firings made Klepper's life miserable, as did some of his cohorts in the PCL. In spite of his business success—or perhaps because of it—the Portland owner had few friends in the game. He was obliged to take Landis to court, where he eventually won based on an obscure Oregon "blue-sky law," which said that no third-party infringement on the state's private investment and property statutes was tolerable, particularly any third party outside the jurisdiction of the Oregon courts. Though he did not conduct business in a manner Landis found laudable, Klepper had not in fact broken any laws other than the baseball commissioner's imaginary ones. Blue-sky laws varied from state-to-state, and still do among those that have them. Oregon's said Klepper was untouchable.

He continued to be ostracized, however, particularly by a few sworn enemies he'd made in the PCL. A faction inside the league also wanted him out of baseball. At the league's executive meetings in 1922, Klepper was involved in a heated argument with Charles Graham and C.H. Straub, officers in the powerful San Francisco Seals organization. Graham had introduced a resolution to bar Klepper from his connection with the Portland club. The two adversaries nearly came to blows in the decorous boardroom where they were meeting and had to be physically separated.

Klepper won his case against Landis in the courts, but like many a man who has had to spend a fortune and endless energy to vindicate him in the American judicial system, he exited the fray tired and disillusioned. No settlement could dispel the ill-will and generally chaotic conditions he'd tolerated as the owner of his first professional baseball team.

In 1924 Landis allowed Duke Kenworthy to return to baseball. Having lost in court to Klepper (the only decision that would go against him in all his time as commissioner), he may have not had a choice. In any case, Klepper put his old friend to work as manager of the 1924 Beavers, replacing popular player/manager Bill Middleton, but fired him halfway through the season as the team languished at the bottom of the PCL standings—despite having future Hall of Fame catcher Mickey Cochrane and Jim Poole aboard.

In Philadelphia for the 1924 World Series, Klepper fell into negotiations with the Athletics' Tom and John Shibe, majority-partners of Connie Mack. Klepper, up to his usual antics, sought to sell Cochrane and Poole to the Athletics. Perhaps the Shibes and Mack were tired of dealing with William Klepper, or perhaps they simply saw an irresistible opportunity.

Whatever precipitated it, the talks soon turned to a different kind of deal. The Shibes offered Klepper $250,000 for the Portland Beavers *and* the ball park they played in—Vaughn Street. The battered owner of the Beavers agreed to the deal and left baseball—for a time.

Portland businessman and civic leader J.W. Cook sponsored the first organized amateur baseball team in Portland, the East Portland Pioneers.

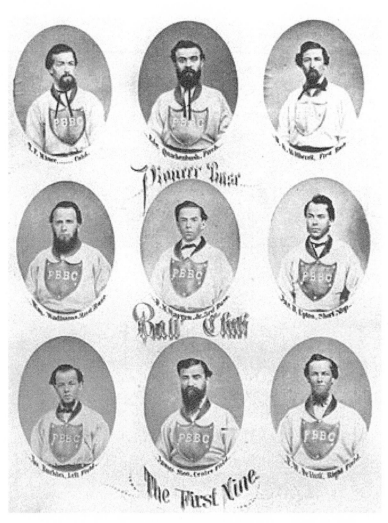

The East Portland Pioneers was the most successful amateur
baseball team in Portland.

JOSEPH BUCHTEL,
PORTLAND, OR.

Joe Buchtel was born in Ohio in 1830. He helped plant the seeds of professional baseball in Portland as player/manager of the East Portland Pioneers and founder of the semi-professional Portland Willamettes.

Joe Tinker began his professional career for William H. Lucas and the Portland Webfoots in Portland in 1901. He quickly moved up to the big leagues the next year.

Former major leaguer William Frederick "Bones" Ely and his
brother Ben Ely purchased the Portland Webfoots from William H.
Lucas and renamed the franchise the Browns in 1903. The Browns
entered the newly formed Pacific Coast League that year.

Judge William McCredie purchased the Portland Browns from the
Ely brothers in 1905 and changed the team's name to the Giants.
He named his nephew, Browns' outfielder Walter McCredie,
manager. A year later, in a vote of the fans, the Giants became the
Portland Beavers and won their first PCL pennant.

Portland manager Walter McCredie won five PCL pennants.

William Klepper would spend a great deal of time and energy feuding with Baseball Commissioner Kenesaw Mountain Landis, during the 1921-24 seasons before selling the Beavers to Connie Mack and the Shibes.

Commissioner Landis came to power on the heels of the 1919 "Black Sox" scandal and vowed to clean up baseball.

Klepper signed catcher Mickey Cochrane for the 1924 season and then sold the future Hall of Famer's contract, along with the rest of the Beavers and Vaughn Street Park, to Philadelphia.

The great Jim Thorpe played part of 1922 with the Beavers before an injury forced him out. Klepper signed him for the then astronomical salary of $1,000 a month.

The legendary Cornelius McGillicuddy (Connie Mack) hired his good friend Thomas L. Turner to run his Portland franchise in 1924.

Mike "Pinky" Higgins hit .328 for the 1932 PCL pennant-winning Portland Beavers. He would become a three-time MLB All-Star (1934, 1936, and 1944) and future Red Sox manager.

Manager Bill Sweeney's Portland Beavers won the 1936 PCL
championship. His uncle, whom he was named for, played with the
Beavers in the1906 championship season.

Ad Liska, whose submarine delivery baffled hitters for 14 seasons in Portland, helped the Beavers win the 1936 and 1945 PCL titles.

Eddie Basinski was a stalwart of the 1945 PCL champs. A highly trained musician, he played violin occasionally with the Portland Symphony and for his enthralled teammates.

Frankie Austin and Luis Marquez became Portland's first black players in 1949 as the PCL followed the lead of Major League Baseball and finally integrated.

Satchel Paige briefly pitched for Portland in 1961. Clay Hopper once managed Jackie Robinson in Montreal.

The 1926 construction of Multnomah Stadium would create a greyhound-racing park. In 1956 the stadium became the new home of the Beavers following the demise of Vaughn Street Park.

Luis Tiant smoking one of his many victory cigars. He went 15-1 for the 1964 Beavers. He returned to Portland on the comeback trail in 1981 to play for David Hersh.

"Sudden" Sam McDowell teamed with Luis Tiant, Steve Hargan and Tom Kelly in 1964 to mow down the PCL. Cleveland called Sam up late in the season and the Beavers lost the PCL crown to the San Diego Padres by one game.

"Sweet" Lou Piniella was a major factor on the 1967 Beavers. Piniella possessed a beautiful swing and a grumpy personality, thus his nickname was both truthful and ironic.

Kurt Russell and his father, Bing, started the Mavericks in 1974.
Kurt played for the Class-A Independent and helped run the team
between acting jobs

The Russells brought Jim Bouton to Portland to pitch for the Mavericks in 1975. The NBC news trucks showed up soon thereafter to film the famous author of *Ball Four*.

Henry Aaron was just one of the many stars David Hersh brought
to Portland in the early 1980s to promote the game. Hersh had a
passionate belief that major-league baseball could happen in
Portland if the politicians and money could get together.
Unfortunately, they never did.

The Tom Turner Years (1925-1934)

On a clear day in any city, and particularly in Portland, with myriad entertainment options available, a man or woman may choose to ignore ball games. Then it will not matter if Pete Rose extends his hitting streak, or how far Willie Stargell hit his long ball yesterday. It will not matter that Don Sutton is about to become the Dodgers' all-time winningest pitcher.

William Klepper sold the Beavers to the Shibe brothers and Connie Mack at the end of the 1924 season. The Shibes then installed Thomas L. Turner as the new team president. Six years later Turner would buy the Beavers outright and become sole owner.

Tom Turner had won a reputation as one of the country's best baseball scouts. His work for the Shibes and Mack had produced dominant teams in Philly for years and would do so residually for the next decade.

Portland was now, for the first time in its history, the official farm team of a major-league organization, though less-formal working arrangements with big-league teams had occasionally existed since the McCredies' era.

As a farm team of Philadelphia, Portland would benefit from Turner's keen eye for talent, but it would also suffer the curse of the minor-league system—player promotion. The arrangement between Philly and Portland produced a constant flow of talented players between the cities. Among those stopping over at Vaughn Street Park on their way to or from the parent organization were Dudley Branom, DeWitt Leborveau, Paul Strand, Bill Bagwell, Frank Sigafoos, Pinky Higgins and Carl Mays, to list just a few.

Portland's fans were accustomed to seeing favorite players come and go, but not at this level of exchange. With the focus of the farm-team system favoring the big club, pennants for the PCL team in Portland were hard to come by. Turner won only one title throughout his Portland years. That was in 1932, his first season as sole owner.

Manager Spencer Abbott's 1932 team counted four outfielders who hit over .300, led by Lou Finney, who hit .351, with 50 doubles. Bob Johnson slammed 29 home runs and hit .330. Fred Berger's 25 home runs and .305 average contributed mightily. The fourth outfielder, Jim Moore, hit .335.

Add to this deep pool the bat and glove of slick-fielding Pinky Higgins, the future three-time Major

League All-Star (.328), and you have a pretty good indication of how good the Beavers were that season.

Testimony to the superior level of competition within the PCL during Turner's era can be introduced in another stat. Sandwiched around the great 1932 campaign were two equally poor ones—1930 and 1934. Both years the Beavers finished in the cellar.

Tom Turner was an eccentric baseball man. When you hear people referring to a player, team manager or executive as a "throwback," they could be describing Turner. Charlie Finley and Ted Turner (no relation) were throwbacks before they became legends for example, because they challenged the conservative status quo in the game. They were big personalities with big ideas, and they didn't care what you thought about them.

In the days before television came to dominate sports, players and management had to mainly deal with sportswriters from the daily papers. Tom Turner seems to have had a rocky relationship with the baseball press.

According to L.H. Gregory, Turner once confronted a group of writers who were badgering him with what he must have felt were inane or unnecessary questions at a local watering hole. He told the writers that he'd just sold the Beavers to a Vancouver, B.C. businessman named Bob Brown. This was the first the writers had heard of the supposed deal—it hadn't even been allowed a rumor stage.

Gregory later wrote that Turner said, with a straight face, "You want a scoop don't you? I just gave you one."

The news sent the writers scurrying back to their offices to write up the story. Later, after the story had been published in its various forms, Bob Brown denied that he'd purchased the Beavers. He'd not talked to Tom Turner about such a transaction. In fact, he'd never met the Portland executive.

Another time, Turner informed a group of writers covering the PCL winter meetings in San Francisco that he'd just purchased the Boston Red Sox.

When the astonished Boston owners denied the story, Turner laughed and shrugged his shoulders.

"You fellows don't have enough to do," he told the writers.

Then there was the time at yet another league meeting when Turner announced his candidacy for governor of Oregon. By then, Gregory wrote in his 1944 reminiscence of the Turner years, the owner's "startling stories" had ceased to be taken seriously.

"How could anyone stay permanently 'mad' at Tom Turner! It was impossible. Down under it all his heart was as big as an apple pie, and just as soft," Gregory wrote, recalling the time in 1929 that Turner paid a full salary to the widow of an unsigned player killed in an auto accident just prior to the season opener.

Big-hearted, jocular Tom Turner wasn't always so kind and funny, however. He had a penchant for hiring and firing managers, employing 10 in as many seasons. He proved his volatility in 1929 when he fired a manager at mid-season and brought in tough-guy Bill Rodgers, who took over with the Beavers mired in the cellar and drove them home to fourth place. The run included a 16-game winning streak late in the season, creating much excitement, big crowds, and the illusion that Turner's reign had finally stabilized.

Throughout the resurgence, Turner gave Rodgers repeated praise for bringing the team back. His words sounded like a daily vote of confidence.

It looked momentarily like Turner had finally found his man. But in the end he fired Rodgers anyway. With the *Great Depression* about to hit, Portland's fans had found more to be depressed about than the economy.

The 1930 season brought a horrific downturn in the economy and the quality of Portland's play. Turner brought in Larry Woodall to replace the popular Rodgers, and Vaughn Street was now graced with lights, making night baseball possible in Portland for the first time.

The changes might have been a boon for the game locally, but the team played so poorly that not even the curiosity of night baseball created much excitement after its novelty wore off. And then there was the matter of the pesky economic situation. At a time when night baseball would theoretically free day workers to attend games as a matter of course, many no longer had jobs and couldn't afford to go.

Hard times and bad baseball combined to indeed make 1930 a miserable year in Portland.

In 1931 things improved for the Beavers on the field as Turner's newest manager, Spencer Abbott, began to assemble the high-powered team that would the following year win the PCL pennant. A fall to fourth in 1933 was followed by the tragic season of Walter

McCredie's return to Vaughn Street. Though sick, he spent the first half of the season managing the Beaver with his old aplomb before falling so ill that he had to finally be hospitalized. Turner and the community organized a tribute for him, hoping to bring him to Vaughn Street for a curtain call. His last request, spoken from his death bed, was that the game and ceremony carry on without him, and that people quickly forget about Walter McCredie.

That last bit wouldn't happen.

Two other significant storylines emerged in Tom Turner's years, both in 1926. That year, Portland employed its first radio broadcaster, and Turner hired full-time groundskeeper Rocky Benevento to groom Vaughn Park. The head groundskeeper for 30 years, Benevento did such a good job that he was as popular among Portland's fans as any of the players—so popular that upon his retirement fans gifted him a new car in appreciation of his good work.

E.J. Schefter, the Return of William Klepper, and Integration (1935-1949)

No promotion, no matter how cleverly conceived, will consistently bring fans into the park to watch an inferior team. If a fan hasn't the time or will to indulge in the gifts of the stars, which is often the case, why think he will be interested in the marginal talents of the minor leagues?

Tom Turner sold the Beavers over the winter of 1934. The buyer was Portland pharmacist E.J. Schefter. His 1935 club had a winning season, finishing one game above .500, a marked improvement after two losing seasons. The next year, 1936, Portland again won the PCL title, narrowly beating out the Oakland Oaks and finishing 96-79. That was the best team Schefter would produce in his tenure as owner.

The Beavers finished fourth in 1937, winning a playoff series against San Francisco before losing to eventual champions San Diego, featuring young phenom Ted Williams. They finished sixth in 1938 before the bottom truly fell out from 1939-1942, cellar-dwelling seasons all. The 1940 team was particularly bad—as in record-setting bad—finishing with a 56-122 record, 25 full games behind the next worst team. The basement had never been more pronounced.

Schefter owned the team for eight seasons before selling it in 1942 to—you guessed it—Judge Kenesaw Mountain Landis' old nemesis, William Klepper.

The resale of the Beavers to Klepper and his new business partner, minority owner George Norgan, marked the return of a man 18 years in exile.

Older and ostensibly wiser, Klepper took over a team that had finished in the cellar three straight seasons and turned it into an immediate winner. Along the way, management and fans took to calling the team the "Lucky Beavers" after numerous close games, and the local media picked up on it. One radio station led a fund-raiser for the war effort that stipulated an American B-52 bomber be given the name "Lucky Beavers." Vaughn Street Park became known as "Lucky Beaver Stadium," in spirit if not officially.

In a league diluted of much of its talent—true throughout baseball, of course—by the war effort, the Beavers finished second in the PCL in 1944.

The 1945 Beavers won another pennant behind manager Marv Owen and the stellar pitching of 20-game winners Ad Liska, Roy Helser and Don Pulford. The community coalesced around the champions and raised funds to present the team with gold and silver rings and commemorative watches. The initiative was organized by writer L.H. Gregory, who thought Portland's 1936 championship team had been under-appreciated and slighted by fans. Oregon Governor Earl Snell presented the rings and watches to the players at a banquet-ceremony in the fancy Multnomah Hotel in downtown Portland.

Klepper finally had his championship. His earlier three-year run as owner of the Beavers had ended in bitterness and defeat, brought on by his own sketchy business practices and the wrath of the Commissioner of Baseball Judge Landis. It must have been an emotional moment for him to finally win it all. Klepper's only regret might have been that Landis had died in 1944 and wasn't around to see his comeback.

Having gotten what he wanted—call it vengeance, in part—Klepper decided to sell the team to his minority partner, George Norgan, at the end of the 1945 season.

The Beavers fell off the pace in 1946, finishing in seventh place and 41 games out of first. The next season Eddie Basinski, one of the most beloved Beavers of all time (he was a literary man and a highly-trained violinist, a graduate of the University of Buffalo music school), joined the team and they jumped to third place, losing to the Los Angeles Angels in the first round of the PCL playoffs. They drew a then-record 421,000 fans to Vaughn Street Park that season. The record would stand until 2001, when the Beavers returned to Portland (after the second of two disappearing acts created by baseball's tenuous minor-league economics) and played in newly renovated Civic Stadium, renamed PGE Park.

In 1948, the year Jackie Robinson became Major League Baseball's first black player, the Beavers finished fifth. The following season, with the color barrier broken at the top, the PCL began its own integration policy. Frankie Austin and Puerto Rico-born Luis Marquez became Portland Beavers. Later, Marquez would become just the fourth Puerto Rican to play in the big leagues.

It is a matter of debate as to when the age of "modern baseball" began. Some say it was when baseball codified the rules throughout the professional game. Others say it began with the founding of the *National Association of Professional Baseball Leagues* or the end of the "dead ball" era. Still others pin it on the "Black Sox" scandal and the hiring of Judge Landis as baseball commissioner to "clean the game up," or the merger of the National and American Leagues into Major League Baseball. In a game as historically rich as baseball, pick your moment.

This writer tends to believe it was the day Jackie Robinson slipped into a Brooklyn Dodgers' uniform.

The 1950s and 1960s

Who is the American baseball fan, and how much will he pay to watch the game? This is the question David Hersh is struggling with today. It's as old as the professional game.

The first four seasons to open the 1950s returned the Portland franchise to mediocrity as the club finished fourth each year, 1950-1954. During that time much was happening both on the field and off, however. In 1952 George Norgan brought in Jackie Robinson's 1946 Montreal Royals' manager, Clay Hopper, to manage the team. Also that year, the PCL sought out and won designation as an "open league" by *NAPBL* in an attempt to become a third major league. In theory the designation moved the PCL a step above its former minor-league status—a move many believed would bring the PCL recognition as a top-tiered league equal in stature to the American and National Leagues.

The future looked bright, but beneath the progressive attitude Portland had a big stadium-logistics problem. By 1953 half-century old Vaughn Street Park was a mess, a victim of several fires and a great deal of vandalism. Plans for a new stadium in the community were first announced by Norgan that year, but he found little support for a community-owned stadium among local politicians and their constituents. As with everything decided by politicians, movement was slow to develop and the Beavers were forced to stay and play amid the ruins of Vaughn Street for another two years.

The fundamental problem of how to finance a baseball-dedicated stadium was never resolved in Portland after Vaughn Street Park's collapse. To this day Portland doesn't have a prime baseball stadium, though Civic Stadium, now Providence Park, once came close. Opportunities to build one have come and gone like tenants in a bad housing project. The area's taxpayers were unwilling to spend to support a new stadium in Portland in the 1950s; the deeper into the twentieth century, the deeper their apathy grew.

Baseball once mattered more to people in general because it was among the few options that entertained in the days before the ubiquity of motion pictures and television, just to name two alternatives that rose to prominence (boating and bowling, anyone?) as minor-league baseball struggled in the entertainment market. Portlanders, never accustomed to the tradition of big-league baseball in their community, were especially susceptible to the growing malaise.

In 1893 affluent members of Portland's two-year-old Multnomah Amateur Athletic Club had built an athletic field to host a variety of club sporting events, including track and field and increasingly popular American-style football. They leased land in the Tanner Creek Gulch area of Southwest Portland that had for years been a Chinese vegetable garden and an important part of the city's food chain, supplying vegetables throughout the region.

The initial construction included a 3,000-seat grandstand and the stadium quickly became a favorite venue for sports-minded Portlanders. Though not conceived as a baseball venue the field did occasionally host professional baseball games, as happened in 1895 when a major-league exhibition game came to town, and again in 1905 when Vaughn Street Park was being used as a track and field facility in conjunction with that year's *Lewis & Clark Exposition and World Fair*.

A major renovation in 1926 expanded the stadium's seating capacity to over 20,000, making it large enough to begin hosting major-college football games. Football never became Multnomah Stadium's staple tenant, but like track and field and the occasional concerts and political events staged there, big-time college games brought in sizeable crowds, creating a very nice revenue stream for the Multnomah Athletic Club.

The Oregon Legislature legalized parimutuel betting in the state in 1931 and a thriving dog racing industry grew up around the Multnomah Kennel Club, which became the stadium's core tenant and remained so for years.

The stadium's seating capacity eventually surpassed Vaughn Street Park's, but the field wasn't permanently configured for baseball until the Beavers were forced to move there in 1956, when George Norgan finally sold dilapidated old Vaughn Street Park to the California Bag and Metal Company on November 1, 1955.

Unable to find proper support for a new stadium among the city's political class, Norgan took the $250,000 he earned on the sale of Vaughn Street Park and left baseball.

For a time, it looked as though baseball might be doomed again in Portland, until locals Cal Souther, Clay Brown, A.B. Graham and Arch Kingsley hit upon a bold idea, floating a "community shares" concept like that of the Green Bay Packers in the National Football League.

Portlanders bought in and saved the franchise. The initial stock sold well, creating 2,400 new owners the first year, and the experiment would survive for the next 14 years. However, when the club went into private ownership again in 1969 the stock was essentially worthless. The club's debt far surpassed its annual revenues.

In 1956, with Vaughn Street Park flattened to make room for more industrial construction in Northwest Portland, the Beavers became permanent tenants of Multnomah Stadium and the greyhound dog racing moved to Portland Meadows in North Portland.

The city took over ownership of the stadium for a cool $2 million in 1966 and renamed it Civic Stadium—a small antidote to the community's general malaise. A bigger idea of building a domed stadium in the Delta Park area of North Portland was floated to taxpayers around that time and was soundly rejected.

Portland filed a $1.8 million lawsuit against Major League Baseball on July 30, 1959, claiming monopoly practices and televised baseball were destroying the minor leagues.

L.H. Gregory covered the story and noted Arch Kingsley's opening salvo: "We have come to the conclusion that redress through the courts is our only hope for saving baseball for the Portland community and for minor-league baseball generally."

The number of minor leagues had dwindled from 61 to 23 in the decade prior to Portland's suit, and in Kingsley's mind the blame rested squarely on the shoulders of Baseball Commissioner Ford Frick, American League President Joe Cronin, and National League President Warren Giles.

Upon hearing of Portland's charges, Frick stated: "Any comment would have to come from attorneys. It looks as if it's another one of those suits filed by Frank Lawrence of Portsmouth, Virginia, which was tossed out of court last February."

The suit dragged on for two years before Portland realized the unlikelihood of victory and dropped it.

The impetus for the suit was likely Major League Baseball's takeover of the PCL's major markets in Los Angeles and San Francisco when the Giants and Dodgers rolled west in 1958.

Cavernous Multnomah Stadium could seat just 30,000. The spanking new concrete and steel superstructures in L.A. and San Francisco could seat 50,000 or more. These modern and sleek homes blew Portland's stadium and others around the country out of the water.

Big money, helped along by friendly taxpayer support for the construction boom in California, told the story as the minor leagues watched helplessly.

Arch Kingsley and the Portland cooperative pushed on. At various time during the 1960s it appeared that the community corporation might survive—even thrive.

In something of a publicity stunt torn out of Bill Veeck's book, the Beavers brought 56 year-old Satchel Paige to Portland for part of the 1961 season. A miracle of longevity, Paige was minimally effective (25 innings and 19 strikeouts, 0 decisions) and far from his old self. The fans came to see him, but the affection didn't last and Paige moved on.

After failing in a 1962-1963 working arrangement with Charlie Finley's Kansas City Athletics, Cleveland's Gabe Paul took the Beavers under his wing. In 1964, the locals actually made a profit.

That year, "Sudden" Sam McDowell and Luis Tiant had a combined 23-1 record before McDowell was called up

100

by the Indians to begin his short, brilliant career as the American League's strikeout leader. Steve Hargan and Tom Kelly rounded out that year's starting rotation, one of the best in Portland's history, perhaps surpassed only by the big three from the 1945 championship season—20-game winners Liska, Helford and Buford.

Without McDowell at season's end, Portland fell one game short of the pennant, losing out to the San Diego Padres on the final day of the season.

With the 1964 team nearly intact the next season, the Beavers won the Western Division PCL title, but lost in the finals.

And in 1967, big guns Lou Klimchock, Jose Vidal, Lou Piniella, Ray Fosse, Richie Scheinblum and Jay Ward led a team that was in last place on 3 July to a tie for first and a playoff spot before losing to Spokane. A nightly average of 12,000 fans watched the Beavers' final five-game home stand that year, a record for sustained attendance, but the figures would ultimately lie about the state of baseball in Portland.

Broke and Struggling (1970s)

This is ridiculous fun, this egg-gathering contest. The parents or guardians of all the kids signed a waiver when they came on the field. Who wants to be libel if one of them gets hurt in the furious action of gathering eggs, a sort of mini free-for-all? Not David Hersh, that is certain.

The community experiment dissolved November 4, 1969 when Portland's baseball stockholders agreed to sell to Cappy Smith, Bob Freitas and local stadium concessionaire, Paul Ail. The sale also ended the sweet working arrangement with Gabe Paul's Cleveland Indians.

Few may have been aware of it at the time, but 1969 would be the beginning of the end of Portland's rich history in Triple-A baseball. The fadeout would be ever so slow, like the end of an epic movie, and remakes and sequels would be attempted with varying degrees of success, but the first, classic 70 years—one might say the meaningful years—were over.

The new owners looked around for a baseball man with the deep experience in the professional game they lacked. They settled on William Cutler, who had worked most recently as a scout for the Montreal Expos and had a combined 20 years of experience as an administrator in the American League, including a stint as vice-president of Charlie Finley's Oakland Athletics. Finley had fired him, but the A's owner was known to be irascible, so that didn't count against the new man. To entice Cutler to come aboard the new owners also gave him a share of the team.

Portland Beavers Inc. lost $30,000 its first season and the three original investors immediately opted out, having had a taste of how difficult it had become in recent years to make a buck in the game. Cutler, a baseball man to the bone, proved to be more resilient. He turned down a job with the Milwaukee Brewers to take over full ownership of the Beavers.

However, in three years trying Cutler couldn't make a go of it in Portland. Those years, 1970-1973, were perhaps the most dismal of the Beavers' long history, both on the field and at the box office. The final season sealed the deal for Cutler as only 92,000 fans paid to get into Civic Stadium. Finally, after 70 years of struggle marked by occasional triumphs and a fair share of failure, the Beavers were seemingly done in Portland. Cutler, because he was the last boss and dared to move the team to Spokane, where he believed both the business climate and fan interest to be superior, became a convenient scapegoat for those old-timers who still remembered the glory days at Vaughn Street.

Bing Russell and the Mavericks

I am standing near the hot dog concession in the left-field bleacher section of Civic Stadium. The hot dogs cost more than the cheap seats here. Hersh is practically giving the tickets away. I wish someone would give me a hot dog.

The Beavers and Triple-A baseball would return in 1978 after a five-year hiatus. In the interim something extraordinary happened. Hollywood producer and actor Bing Russell, who had both business acumen and a flair for public relations—and not coincidentally a young son who played baseball—saw opportunity in Portland in 1973, whereas others saw hopelessness and long rainy seasons.

The elder Russell had also once played minor-league baseball, so he was far from naïve about what he was doing.

Bing Russell verily danced into town like a musical actor dancing across a Broadway stage, drawing the media and Portland's baseball fans toward his well-honed act. He paid the Class-A Northwest League for the territorial rights to the Portland market and created the Portland Mavericks, an Independent organization that he and son Kurt would build from scratch. Without the affiliation of a major-league team to provide them players the Russells and their first manager, Hank Robinson, held a tryout at Civic Stadium and put together a ragtag team of washed up ex-minor leaguers, and one very important ex-big leaguer with a poison pen. Many of them demonstrated a surprising ability to still play, including a few who had long been out of the game.

Russell enjoyed enormous success in Portland and made a profit every year. Fully committed to creating a fun atmosphere and putting on a nightly show for the fans, he brought in his kind of actors—showbiz types who knew the game, starting with his son, whose acting career was just taking off. Hank Robinson played minor-league baseball for years before turning to acting; others would become actors after the Mavericks' time, using their connections with Russell to get into the acting game. Kurt Russell played the inaugural season before his career took him away from the game until he made a brief reappearance during the final 1977 Maverick season.

Eccentric former Oregon State star and journeyman in the Baltimore Orioles organization, Frank Peters, managed the Mavs for part of one season. Peters would later do a 30-month stretch of hard time in the Oregon State Penitentiary for growing and selling marijuana, among other charges. He had made a name for himself as a bar owner in Portland and Seattle after his playing career and once ran for governor of Oregon. They called him "The Flake." He described himself as *Machiavellian*, which has a certain honest sound for a politician.

But Russell's biggest coup was signing former Yankee knuckleballer Jim Bouton to play for him in 1975. Bouton was famous for both his wicked knuckler and his own eccentricities, which were well-documented in *Ball Four*, the best-selling baseball expose he'd penned with sportswriter Leonard Schechter in 1970. Bouton didn't have a lot of friends in baseball after publication. People were understandably mad at him for revealing a side of baseball not often glimpsed by non-insiders. The writer Bouton had tattled on people and taken others to task.

But Bouton was a hero to those hungry for his kind of story—a glimpse of the truth—and Russell knew it. Bouton had been out of baseball for five years, but his time in Portland reinvigorated his career and helped land him a contract with the Atlanta Braves in 1978.

Also during his time here he and teammate Rob Nelson hit upon a brainstorm and began marketing a bubble gum as *Big League Chew*.

NBC's Joe Garagiola brought a film crew to Portland to cover the entertaining story of the Mavericks and Bouton's role on the team, which happened to be just the sort of public relations Russell was seeking when he brought the biggest maverick of them all to Portland.

A new film about the halcyon Maverick years, *The Battered Bastards of Baseball*, appeared in the 2014 Sundance Festival. Featuring interviews with some of the Maverick organization's stalwarts, including Kurt Russell, Todd Field, Rob Nelson and Frank Peters, the 73 min. film is garnering excellent reviews at the time of this writing.

In a lot of people's minds the Mavericks disappeared too soon. They were entertaining and also played good baseball, winning four Northwest League divisional titles in five seasons, though the overall league championship eluded them.

At the end of the 1977 season the PCL and Leo Ornest reclaimed Portland for Triple-A baseball, but not before Russell balked and took them to court. He won what he called a "comfortable and satisfactory" settlement for his trouble, but the rights to the territory were "grandfathered" back to the PCL.

Ornest's Beavers made the league playoffs in his first and only season in Portland, but in a telling slight to fans the PCL cancelled them due to inclement weather.

No waiting for the sun to reappear. Everybody had better things to do when it rained.

Ornest stayed a year before the Beavers moved again and David Hersh stepped into the scene.

Memories of the Philadelphia Kid

As I walk from the hollow interior of Civic Stadium, the KXL disc jockey who emceed the egg hunt is taking testimonials from the lucky winners. He pulls aside a very happy youngster and talks to him about the thrill of it all.

Note: This chapter is adapted from "Henry Aaron" by Buddy Dooley, from *People, Polemics & Pooh-Pah: Notes from Under the Bar* (Round Bend Press Books, 2011) and used with permission of the author.

In **1980 I** researched and wrote a series of historical pieces on the Portland Beavers while working for a community monthly in Northwest Portland. I dug into a trove of microfiche files at the Portland library to find material dating from turn-of-the-century newspapers, and I leaned heavily on many stories by a long-time *Oregonian* writer, a legend in Oregon named L.H. Gregory, whom I could remember reading as a kid.

Gregory was among the last of the old-time sportswriters. He referred to the ball players as "lads" and extolled their virtues as "fine young men," and once described a manager as having a "Romanesque stature and nose," a man whose "dignity" surpassed even his managerial skills, etc.

A night on the town would include players under Gregory's watchful gaze "ice-skating in Fresno" on an off day, and "cutting manly figures" as they circled around the rink and "impressed the local ladies."

It was good stuff, but I always wondered if he was serious.

I used as much of the material as I could find and put together six pieces covering professional baseball in Portland between 1901 and 1980.

Lo, I had a minor hit in the community! People, generally old men, but a few old women as well, wrote to the newspaper thanking us for the memories of Vaughn Street Park, Portland's home field for over fifty years. Built in 1901, Vaughn had once been the finest ball park on the West Coast, people said. *Everything changed when they tore that old stadium down in 1955. It just wasn't the same.*

Baseball is American society's biggest nostalgia hook, even when the nostalgia is phony and trumped up by the game's never-ending self-promotion. Or by George Will, the waxiest of the baseball philosophers.

I understood baseball because I played the game. I played Little League, Babe Ruth, high school and junior college ball. But I swear to God baseball doesn't make me nostalgic at all. In fact, I care a lot less for the game today than I did in 1980. It's too money-centric now, and as with every professional sport many of the players are all about the money and little else. When Curt Flood sued baseball to free players at the negotiating table, the game changed, and not just the ball parks, which always get rickety and old.

Though unsuccessful in his suit, Curt Flood started free-agency rolling. That was good for the players, but bad for the fans. I knew Pete Ward, who played for the White Sox and Yankees for a decade, from my work in the bar business. He was a beer rep for a Portland distributor when I met him, and we once talked about the big money that came into baseball after he retired. He seemed a little wistful about the entire situation.

The baseball strike in the 1990s was the last straw for me. I'm not the fan I used to be. Honestly, the game often bores me to death now, in part because I don't have the interest one must have to keep up with the revolving door of trades and salary disputes and drunken driving charges and dugout tiffs and on and on.

Throw in the "juicing" controversies of recent years and you have a yawner.

I wrote my six articles about the Beavers, and then I essentially lost interest in the team. Over the ensuing years I watched a handful of games and I didn't miss baseball at all.

In 1979 the Beavers switched hands again, this time falling in the lap of a young, aggressive Philadelphia native named David Hersh. Hersh favored long, thick, expensive cigars and nicely tailored suits and had a promoter's sensibility, like Charlie Finley, the then owner of the Oakland A's, and like one of the game's greatest-ever promoters, Bill Veeck (*as in wreck*).

Veeck, owner of the Chicago White Sox, made an early name for himself in 1951 when he hired 3' 7" Eddie Gaedel to pinch hit against the Detroit Tigers. The opposing pitcher walked him, of course, unable to find the six-inch strike zone a hunched over "little person" presents. For his part, Finley kept a mule as a mascot at the ball park in Oakland, a proud symbol of his stubborn personality they say. Finley's teams were the first to wear white shoes, and the owner thought, strangely, that orange baseballs might enhance the game.

David Hersh was 23 when he came to Portland in 1979.

Never mind his relative inexperience, Hersh had somehow managed to find a list of investors who backed his dream, for a while, of placing Major League Baseball in Portland within a few years.

Like orange baseballs, it didn't happen, and Hersh moved on, dashing the hopes of Portland's smattering of hardcore fans.

I liked Hersh for his brashness and early willfulness to get it done and bring big-league baseball to Portland. The Triple-A Beavers were good, but there is a considerable fall-off between the second highest level of baseball and the pinnacle league Ruth and Gehrig helped build while nailing the grandstands together in Yankee Stadium. Anyone who knows baseball understands this, so the excitement Hersh brought to town was tangible.

I met Hersh at the stadium, where I'd been summoned by his director of communications. The organization was interested in my baseball history. I let them use whatever text they wanted to promote the team in their program, and in return they issued me a press pass, which I used sporadically for the next couple of seasons. I had asked for money, and director said, "We're not *that* interested!"

The pass gave me access to the press box behind home plate, where I sat and daydreamed throughout the few games I attended. I may have even fallen asleep on occasion, to tell you how interested I was in the proceedings. I didn't write any more baseball stories that year.

Hersh walked up and down press row at times, doling out free food to the writers, which must have included me because when I was there I ate really well. Big, tasty sandwiches and all the pizza I wanted. Plus salads and savory desserts, cakes, trays of donuts, veggie plates—damn, I'm getting hungry recalling it all.

Hersh was a hand-shaker of course, moving around the ball park in an effort to meet as many paying customers as he could. He was a back-slapper, touchy-feely, and he laughed at poor quips—an honest to God salesman spreading his warm dreams to the writers and fans in the sincerest terms, with a perfect white smile, billowing cigar smoke as he strolled.

Hersh the promoter had worked out an affiliate-agreement with the Pittsburgh Pirates, the team he brought to town for an exhibition at mid-season his first year. He held a home run contest, and the sight of Willie

Stargell hitting the ball over 500 ft. to the Multnomah Athletic Club balcony overlooking the ball park in right field *was* an unforgettable sight, it really was. Hersh, smoking his cigar, stood near the on-deck circle with a wad of hundreds in his fist, and every time Stargell or the other derby contestants hit one out the kid would make a show of giving the batter a hundred. Two hours of this during pre-game, and the tab ran into the thousands.

A year or two later, Hersh brought Mickey Mantle and Henry Aaron to town for a special promotion. I heard later that Mick had been in Joe's Cellar on 21st Ave. with other baseball-types the night before and had drank a few and made an ass out of himself, which might explain why I didn't see him at the park the next night.

But I'm not absolutely sure he wasn't there; all I know is he didn't make it down to the press box, or I didn't see him at any rate.

I ran into Aaron after the game. The stadium offices were under the grandstands and I was down there, had just turned a corner out of the press box and I practically walked into Hammerin' Hank.

You know, Aaron wasn't a very large man, which was surprising given the number of homers he hit—755.

They say his power came from his wrists. When I saw Hank I naturally looked at those wrists, and I said, "Hello, Mr. Aaron."

He nodded and kept moving, until I said, "Could you please sign this for me?" I was holding a scrap of paper I'd just ripped from my notebook.

Hank looked at me with curious discernment and said, "Aren't you a little old to be asking for an autograph?"

Perhaps I was at 29. After that I don't remember what else I said, or how I justified myself to the great Hank Aaron, but he signed.

I owned that autograph for 20 years before losing it in a move, unfortunately.

New Partners and the End of the Dream

"And what did you win, young man?"
"I won a $200 color-television set," the kid yelled.
"How do you feel about that?"
"Lucky!"

Hersh needed cash after giving all of his to the home run derby contestants. Enter Portland automobile sales mogul Ron Tonkin and City Center Parking millionaire Ron Goodman, who sweetened the pot for Hersh in his second season and purchased majority control of the team.

The four-year affiliation with the Pittsburgh Pirates ended in 1982 as Tonkin and Goodman were able to talk their friends in city hall into renovating tired, old Civic Stadium at last. It was a limited, quickie job and gave the structure a badly needed new roof, new artificial turf, and row upon row of sturdy, auditorium-style seating.

In 1983, the Beavers switched affiliations, inking a pact with the star-studded Philadelphia Phillies in the days before Pete Rose's gambling issues earned the wrath of Baseball Commissioner Bart Giamatti. On the job just six-months before a fatal heart attacked felled him at age 51, baseball's seventh commissioner would give Rose a lifetime ban from the game, upholding the squeaky-clean philosophy of the game introduced by Judge Landis.

In baseball, no cheating is allowed—ever. Well, unless it involves performance enhancing drugs, which merit a slap on the wrist and brief suspensions. Had baseball banned everyone involved in the "juicing" scandals of recent times, the effect would have been like that of World War II on baseball—extreme dilution of the product.

The 1983 Beavers won another PCL pennant, reflecting the talent level that flowed between Philly and Portland that season

Joe Buzas bought the Portland Beavers from Tonkin and Goodman at the close of the 1983 season. Out the door with them went David Hersh's big dream. The kid himself returned to the East Coast.

Buzas immediately had the absurd idea of renaming the team the Portland Phillies, a decision that ignored the long tradition of the team's favored name. The fans shouted him down, explaining they were well-aware of the Philadelphia affiliation and that he need not be rash.

Of all the wheelers and dealers who came through Portland, New Jersey-raised Buzas was perhaps one of the most unique, given his voluminous penchant for buying, moving, and selling baseball franchises. The one-time Yankee shortstop (30 career games) became a manager in Puerto Rico at 26. Ten years later he bought his first team, the Class-A Allentown, PA Red Sox. He would go on to operate 82 organizations in 45 years in the baseball business.

Buzas moved the Portland team to Salt Lake City in 1994 and changed its name to the *Buzz* (later renamed *Bees*) and apparently nobody objected this time. His Salt Lake team thrived, leading the PCL in attendance during its first six seasons in town.

Once again bereft of PCL Triple-A baseball, the Portland market opened its arms to Jack Cain and his Class-A Bend Rockies in 1995. Affiliated with the Colorado Rockies, as the name implies, the Northwest League team won the title in 1997 and drew well enough that Cain was, like Bing Russell 20 years earlier, able to parlay his success into a nice payday in 2000 when once again the PCL came calling to reclaim the territory.

Another face lift to Civic Stadium and additional taxpayer-paid structural repairs ensued, with the addition of "luxury boxes," new turf and a beer garden. Civic Stadium became PGE Park. (Portland General Electric is what it sounds like, an energy corporation.) It was likely not a coincidence that the "the smartest guys in the room" from Enron, which had recently purchased PGE, were infiltrating Portland at the time, having already played the name-the-stadium game in Houston. Enron Park is no more of course, and neither is Enron. Nor is PGE Park.

Somehow throughout all of this PGE (the company) survived; however, a few of its officers got into a little trouble.

The new Portland Triple-A team moved to town from Albuquerque. The New Mexico franchise in turn had once been the original Los Angeles Angels, a charter member of the 1903 PCL. This time, the major-league affiliate was the San Diego Padres and Portland enjoyed baseball for the next decade. A nice beer garden along the refurbished stadium's first-base line helped the cause, as "Thirsty Thursdays" became the rage. On those evening the discounted craft beer flowed like the Willamette River, and those adventurous enough to take in a game at the beautiful facility enjoyed themselves to the fullest.

Burp.

Merritt Paulson purchased the Beavers in 2007. Like Joe Buzas before him, he didn't really like the name of the team. He thought it might be confused with the Oregon State mascot of the same name. Never mind that it was only out-of-towners like himself who might have that problem. Thus, he borrowed the century-old gambit of taking the issue to the public, like the McCredies had when they discarded the Giants moniker.

This time the voting happened at the team's spanking-new website and Paulson received his first reality check about baseball tradition in Portland. The Beavers won.

Ultimately it wouldn't matter, however. Paulson's real interest was soccer, the international killjob that is the face of corporate globalization mingled with a little hooliganism. You see, along with the baseball team, Paulson purchased the city's soccer franchise, the very popular Portland Timbers.

He didn't even try to change the name of that outfit.

It remains a matter of debate about just how interested Paulson was in keeping the baseball part of his enterprise in business. His avowed goal from the start was to turn the Timbers into a Major League Soccer franchise. Original plans called for the third renovation of PGE Park into what became Jeld-Wen Field, a soccer-dedicated stadium seating 20,000. (Timbers' matches sell out regularly and the region's soccer fans are mad for them, so Paulson knew what he was doing.) To accomplish this, Paulson worked with the city, half-heartedly seeking out a site for a new baseball stadium large enough to accommodate the Beavers, or as some fans yet hoped, a future MLB team. Numerous sites fell through or were never seriously considered. At one point the Montreal Expos, who were preparing to leave Canada, held talks with interested persons in town who had the desire, if not the money, to keep baseball in Portland.

The Expos were also talking with Washington, D.C., which took the game seriously and found the money to build a new stadium. After months of talks, the Expos became the Washington Nationals.

Paulson's original deal with Portland stipulated that both the Timbers and Beavers would be a part of the future. But the big money couldn't be found and in the end the Portland City Council, led by Mayor Sam Adams and Councilman Randy Leonard, let Paulson off the hook as he agreed to pay for a great deal of the Jeld-Wen Field renovations.

Paulson didn't have the extra money or likely the sincerest interest in paying for a baseball park.

Neither did anyone else. The Beavers played their final game at PGE Park on September 6, 2010.

The game sold out and soon thereafter Paulson sold the team to a group in Tucson.

The Jeld-Wen Corp. went bankrupt and the stadium found a new sponsor for the 2014 MLS season.

An old-timer wouldn't know the old Civic Stadium the way Providence Park looks today. There isn't a baseball to be found there.

Will the Beavers ever return? Who knows? Another question might be: Does anybody care?

Sources

Newspapers

The *Oregon Journal*

The *Oregonian*

Websites and Links

http://en.wikipedia.org/wiki/Portland_Beavers

http://en.wikipedia.org/wiki/History_of_baseball_in_Po
rtland,_Oregon

http://www.pdxhistory.com/html/portland_baseball.ht
ml

http://www.scottymoore.net/portland57.html

Note: Where quotes are used the author has identified
the specific source in the text.

Other Round Bend Press books by Terry Simons

Alt-Everything (Essays)
A Marvelous Paranoia (Memoir)
Four Absurd Plays
Cold Eye: A Generation of Voices (Poetry Anthology, Ed.)
Two Stories (Chapbook)
Cello Music & Other Poems (Chapbook)
Of Dirty Kitchens, Bedlam & the Bomb (Essay)
People, Polemics & Pooh-Pah (with Buddy Dooley)

To view the full catalog of Round Bend Press books see our website: roundbendpressbooks.blogspot.com.

Made in the USA
Las Vegas, NV
20 February 2023

67819336R00080